*This book is dedicated to all
of the future changemakers.
May you make ripples of kindness,
justice, and peace in this world,
no matter how small. -LF*

Published and written by Leigh Anne Fortner
Text Copyright © 2022 by Leigh Anne Fortner
Illustrations Copyright © 2023 by Anastassiya Selezneva

All rights reserved. No part of this publication may be reproduced, distributed, or transmitted in any form or by any means, including photocopying, recording, or other electronic or mechanical methods, without the prior written permission of the author, except in the case of brief quotations embodied in critical reviews and certain other non-commercial uses permitted by copyright law.

Paperback ISBN: 978-1-7378414-4-9
Hardcover ISBN: 978-1-7378414-3-2
Ebook ISBN: 978-1-7378414-5-6

www.spreadthelightbooks.com

Publisher's Cataloging-in-Publication data
Names: Fortner, Leigh Anne, author. | Selezneva, Anastassiya, illustrator.
Title: Ripples / written by Leigh Anne Fortner; illustrated by Anastassiya Selezneva.
Description: Conway, AR: Leigh Anne Fortner, 2023. | Summary: A young girl observes ripples forming on the lake and is inspired to create her own ripples of kindness and love in the world.
Identifiers: LCCN: 2022923427 | ISBN: 978-1-7378414-3-2 (hardcover)
978-1-7378414-4-9 (paperback) | 978-1-7378414-5-6 (ebook)
Subjects: LCSH Change (Psychology)--Juvenile fiction. | Kindness--Juvenile fiction.
| BISAC JUVENILE FICTION / Science & Nature / General | JUVENILE FICTION / Social Themes / Values & Virtues
Classification: LCC PZ7.1 .F67 Ri 2023 | DDC [E]--dc23

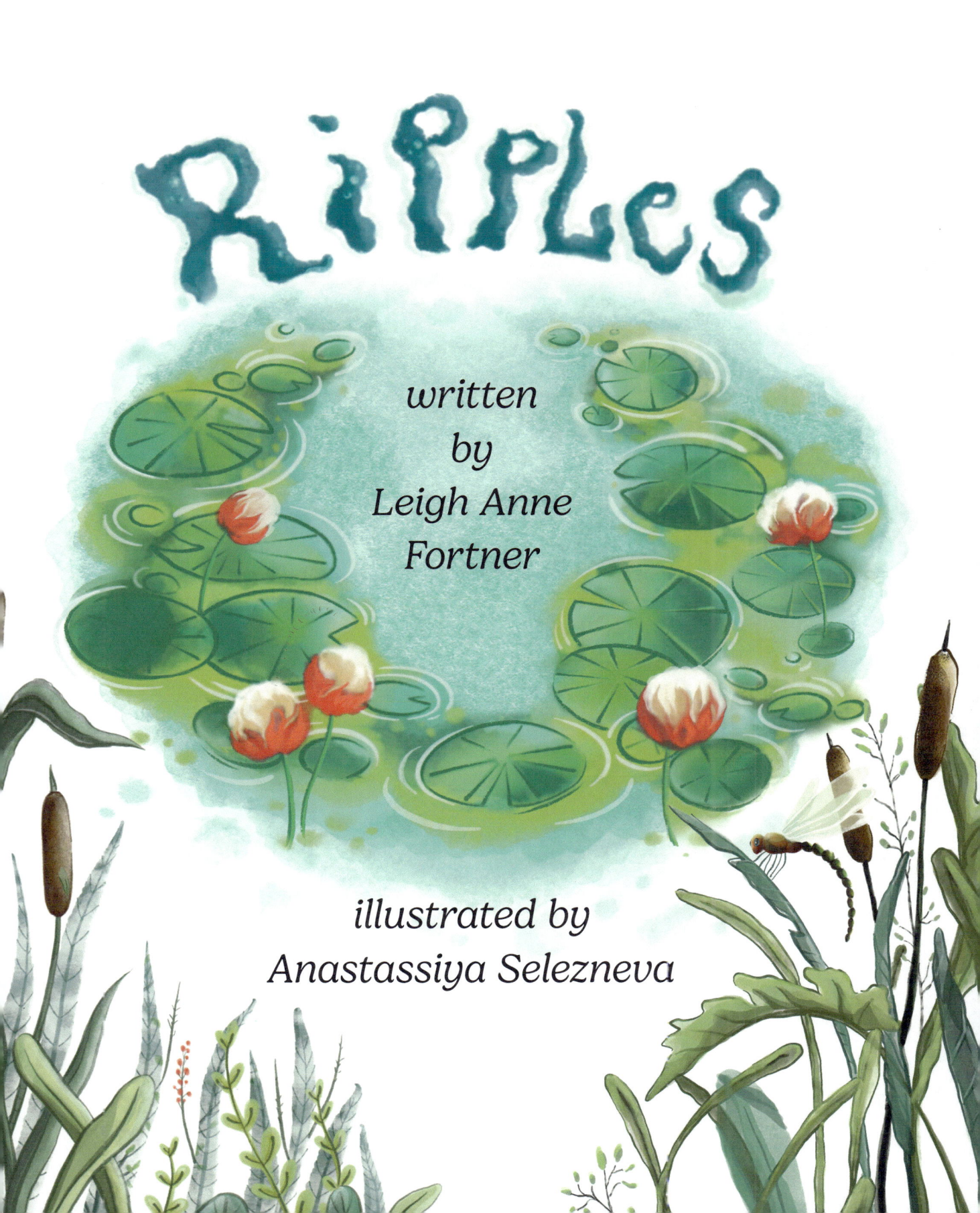

Plop

One tiny drop.
The rain starts, and I see it...

It moves out,
Its rings growing bigger,

changing
the surface of
the lake
as it expands.

Plop
Plop
Plop

The rain comes down faster now,
and the ripples all seem to dance together,
each one changing the next
until you can no longer
tell them apart.

One tiny thought.
An idea!
My brain goes wild with the possibilities. "If a drop of rain can make an entire lake dance, then what will this small idea change?"

One tiny seed. Into the dirt, I drop it. Then seed after seed, I plant them, covering each carefully with dirt, and sprinkling with water.

Each day
the flowers grow
bigger and bigger,
reaching up towards
the light...
until the bright
yellow petals form a
perfect circle
as bright as the sun.

I cut each flower and carefully wrap
them into little bundles to share,
hoping that my own ripples
can move mountains.

"Excuse me, sir."

"What do you want?" replies a burly man in uniform.

"Ripples,"

I say reluctantly.
"I just want
to start ripples."
I hand him
the bouquet.

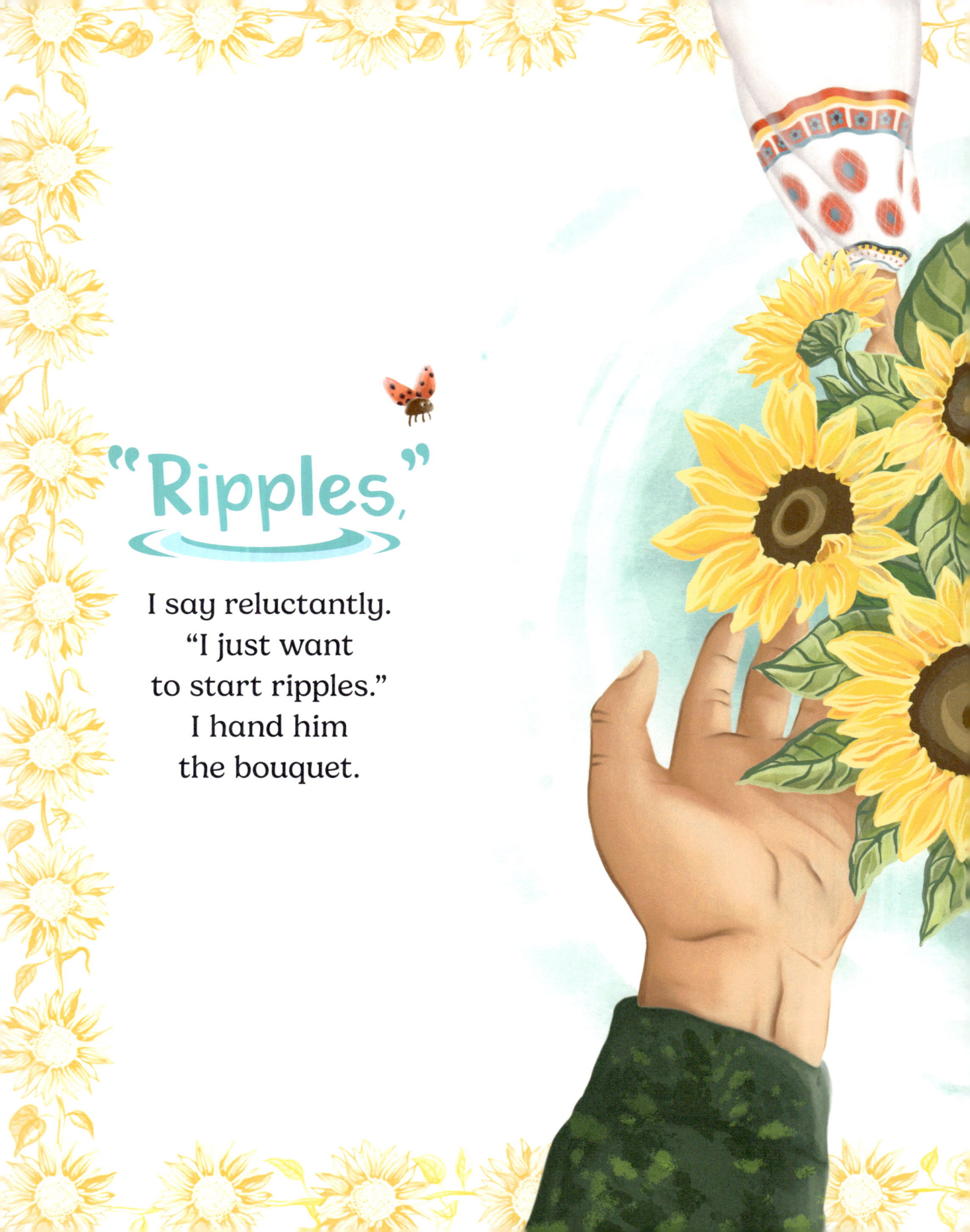

His harsh stare
turns soft
for a moment.
He takes
the flowers and
looks away.

This book was written on the day Russia invaded Ukraine. The illustrations and themes of this book were created to honor the people of Ukraine and to provide children with hope for a better future. At Spread The Light Books, we believe in creating beautiful stories that give back to the community. That is why all net proceeds of this book will be donated to Liberty Ukraine, a non- profit organization committed to providing humanitarian aid, medical supplies, protective gear, and rehabilitative therapy to the people of Ukraine. If you would like to learn more about how to directly contribute to this organization, please visit

www.libertyukraine.org.

Now, It's Your Turn!
Pick an idea from this list, or come up with your own ideas
to create some ripples.

 Draw a picture and give it to someone to show you care.

 Bake cookies and give them to someone as a sweet surprise.

 Look for a kid who is all alone at recess and invite them to play with you.

 Set up a lemonade or hot cocoa stand. Then donate the money you make to a local charity.

 Volunteer at your local food bank or animal shelter.

 Host a game day at a local retirement center or nursing home.

 Smile and give a compliment to a stranger at the grocery store.

 When you outgrow some of your clothes or toys, donate them to someone in need.

 Help the earth by recycling.

 Give this book as a gift to someone to spread the message further.

Have a grown up share your *ripples* by taking a picture
and tagging @spreadthelightbooks on Instagram.
We can't wait to see what you do!

Leigh Anne Fortner

is a Speech-Language Pathologist and children's book author. Her knowledge of language and childhood development, combined with her creativity, has enabled her to produce heart-warming stories that inspire young children to learn and grow. Leigh Anne hopes to create a positive impact on others by donating all net proceeds from her books to non-profits in her community and beyond. She resides in Conway, Arkansas and is the mother of two little bookworms.

Visit Instagram
@spreadthelightbooks or
www.spreadthelightbooks.com
to learn more.

If you enjoyed this story, please leave a positive review on Amazon or GoodReads. Reviews are greatly appreciated and will help others discover this story.

Interested in more?
Scan the QR code to visit the author's website, grab free resources, and check out more books that give back.

Made in United States
Troutdale, OR
11/13/2024

24750351R00019